MY
GARDENING
JOURNAL

TABLE
OF CONTENTS

Introduction___4

PART I: A BEGINNER'S GUIDE TO GARDENING___10

Getting Started___12

Recommended Tools___13

Ten Steps to a Successful Garden___14

How to Determine What Will Succeed in Your Garden___16

Transplants vs. Seed-Starts___20

How to Start Seeds Indoors___26

Common Gardening Terms___34

A Few Final Thoughts___48

PART II: PLAN YOUR GARDEN___50

Sun Tracker___52

Garden Planning Grids___54

Seasonal Chores Tracker___58

PART III: PLANT LOGS___62

PART IV: WEEKLY GARDENING JOURNAL___78

Additional Resources___184

INTRODUCTION

Some of us cannot help but get our hands in the dirt; many of us long for that kind of passion, but we are just looking for the spark. Maybe we want to dig deep in the earth of our own backyard because we know instinctively that we will simultaneously dig deep inside ourselves as we learn, push, and grow. Like all good growth, it takes time. Gardening is a journey that can span many years, with many seasons inside of those years. The seasons, in turn, are made of days and hours and minutes that will pass regardless of what we choose to do with them. Investing our time and attention into the garden is an invitation to pause, observe, reflect, take note, celebrate, and savor. What could be a worthier pursuit than this to fill our moments?

*Pause, observe, reflect,
take note, celebrate, and savor.*

We have been building, planting, sowing, pruning, and harvesting in our little quarter-acre urban garden in Seattle, Washington for more than a decade. When we first found our home, there was one magnolia tree and not much else. We had a blank canvas to play with, and we have learned, dreamed, fretted, and played so much since. It's a delight to sit side-by-side today and remember the past seasons when we planted hedges, built new garden beds, or tried growing a new crop.

Together we have tracked the dates of our region's first and last frost, made note of when to harvest the kale from one season to the next, and observed when the roses were at the most beautiful bloom. We have paid attention to which birds seem to enjoy frequenting specific areas. We have wondered, what plants are flourishing? What needs a bit more help next time? Taking a daily garden stroll marks one day from the next and by musing over the changes and documenting our hard-won lessons, we naturally grew in our knowledge as the garden grew in beauty.

Every day you dig in the earth, you learn something new, and there are so many simple joys and pleasures to be found in one's own plot of earth! Welcome, you are here, and it's a perfect season to begin.

WHY A GARDEN JOURNAL?

This journal is your invitation to dig deep (pun intended, of course). A careful attention to detail forces us to slow down and observe, two important characteristics of a happy gardener. When we record something, we have marked it as special! The simple act of writing a few notes on what you've noticed allows your delight in the garden to deepen. Maybe it's the first blossoms on stone fruit trees or the day your first snowdrop flower pushes its way forth as the herald of spring. Maybe you want to write down dates that your garden is in her prime form so you can remember to schedule a little garden party during this time next year. Maybe you want to track the percentage of seeds that reached maturity and which plants you'll sow as transplants next season. Are there any patches where it's warm enough to go out and enjoy sitting amongst your flowers, or any pests that have made themselves known so you can collect your

neighbor's advice on how to handle them? Some days in the garden will be much busier than others, and making note of the weeks of heavy harvest or weeding can prepare you for the next season.

As you daydream about the future, sketch out possible vegetable and herb plant layouts. Take photos of your garden in different seasons and add them to these pages (you will be amazed at the changes from one week to the next!). Slowly but surely, not only will this become a practical journal for your unique garden but also a diary of your creative art form, a wonderful guide to reference for future seasons, and a helpful manual for others who would like to know about your successes and lessons learned.

IN PART I, you'll find our best tips, tricks, and lessons that every beginner gardener needs to know to grow a successful garden. This includes our recommendations for gardening tools, a list of easy plants to grow if you're new to gardening, and tips for starting seeds indoors, among many other helpful lessons.

PART II provides space to properly plan your garden, including a chart to track the levels of sunlight your yard receives, grids to sketch out your dream garden layout, and lines to write a bucket list for your garden—like which vegetables, fruits, herbs, and flowers you dream of growing.

PART III includes dozens of plant logs, where you can keep track of each plant you grow and how much light and space it needs, when it needs to be planted, and how long until it's ready to harvest.

FINALLY, IN PART IV, we've provided a weekly gardening journal for you to track the progress of your plants, write observations for your next growing season, and remind yourself of important gardening tasks to complete throughout the year.

Gardening is much like any practice in that so much goes on behind the scenes for the majority of the time, and a lot of it is not what many consider glamorous. However, a harvest of plenty only comes after much work has been invested. Just like anything that's worth pursuing, success comes with the common denominators of time and patience. Gardening, friendships, painting, a good slow-cooked meal—we love to experience and reap the benefits of these beautiful things, but they all begin with investing time and a lot of not-always-pretty moments. Starting with an attitude of hope gets you miles ahead of the weeds. Remember to give yourself grace as you learn. Again and again. The passion deepens, knowledge and wisdom expand, and an unexpected bloom—delight! Like all good things, gardening is the very best when the harvest is shared. Thank you for letting us share our experience, and this journal, with YOU. We cannot wait to hear about your garden and see how you use this journal throughout the seasons to come.

Sarah + Colin

Part One

A BEGINNER'S GUIDE
TO GARDENING

GETTING STARTED

Are you ready to start planning your garden? It's time to think about the adventure that awaits you in the seasons to come. Your plants are only as healthy as their home; after all, they cannot simply get up and relocate. To begin, you must consider your garden space. Perhaps you simply have a large container in your apartment and this is your first foray into urban gardening. Or maybe you have a little bit of earth and you're ready to sow some seeds. For all types of space, the forethought is the same and follows this framework: know your space, sunlight, soil, and south-facing garden spots.

- **SPACE**: Plants have different space requirements, both in depth and width. What kind of space do you have to share with plants?

- **SUNLIGHT**: Most plants need 6+ hours of direct sunlight per day, with vegetables being the most sunlight dependent. Track the hours of sunlight each area receives in your garden using the Sun Tracker charts on page 52.

- **SOIL**: Growing healthy plants begins with the composition of the earth in which you sow. Healthy roots transfer nutrients from the soil to your plants, so healthy soil equals healthy plants. Soil is also responsible for water retention, so your soil may need to be well-draining, depending on your plants' needs. As you begin to dream about what to grow in your garden, begin to note each plant's unique soil needs.

- **SOUTH-FACING**: Your plants like this direction the best! Use this journal to make note of the directions the areas in your garden face and make sure you've got some great south-facing areas in mind.

Another helpful hint: Just like plants, we are so much better in a community. Visit your local nurseries or speak with neighbors to get your questions answered. The online gardening community is thriving too! Follow local florists, gardeners, and farmers on social media. Observe what they grow and share . . . and get ready to make some new friends because plant people *love* to talk about plants!

RECOMMENDED TOOLS

Here are a few of our suggestions for tools you may need as you begin your garden. Depending on the space you have or the plants you want to grow, you may or may not need all of these items.

Small- to Medium-Sized Gardens:

- Spade/trowel for weeding and digging
- Shovel
- Gloves
- Plant markers
- Watering wand and nozzle
- Knee pad
- Gardening shears
- Gathering bucket or basket for collecting weeds, carrying tools, and harvesting plants as you move around your garden

Larger Gardens:

- Wheelbarrow
- Rake
- Plant supports, like garden twine, stakes, or bamboo canes
- Soaker hose, stakes for hose, and a timer for watering
- If you have limited space, go vertical: consider a trellis for sweet peas!

Extra Fancy Tidbits We Enjoy in Our Garden

- Japanese Hori Hori digging knife
- Floret Farm's tool belt

TEN STEPS TO A SUCCESSFUL GARDEN

You are ready to begin—you have committed and you're holding this journal in your hopeful hands. Now what? You've observed your gardening space, making note of the space, sunlight patterns, soil conditions, and south-facing spots that your plants will prefer.

Step 1: The first step to beginning a garden is to map out your space—in this journal! Be sure to include existing structures and any landscape elements. Use the grid paper starting on page 54 to measure and sketch it out. Now, how to figure out the best spot to add your garden . . .

Step 2: Once your space is mapped out, you can begin to observe which areas of your yard get the most sunlight. Wait for a clear, sunny day and make note of how the sun moves throughout your space. Using the Sun Tracker charts on page 52, record the time when a potential garden area starts getting sun and what time it gets shaded. Each spot doesn't need to receive continuous sunlight, but ideally, each area will get at least 6 hours of sun exposure every day. Different plants are going to have different needs, and once you have the areas of your yard mapped out, it will be easier to determine which plants will thrive in your garden.

Step 3: Know your soil. The best way to do this is to get a soil test kit so you can determine the health of your soil, as well as the soil pH.

Step 4: Learn your plant hardiness zone, climate, and first and last frost dates. See page 16 to determine your region's unique requirements.

Step 5: Dream and scheme. Based on everything you've learned so far, it's now time to decide what to grow. What do you want to sow? Maybe you'd prefer a cut flower garden to make fresh bouquets, or perhaps you're dreaming of an herb garden you can browse through and snip fresh for meals. Or perhaps you'd like to try your hand at growing vegetables to supplement your meals. Based on your dreams for this upcoming year's garden and the knowledge you now have of your unique space, it's time to jot down and research your ideas for the right plants to tend to. If your space is limited, narrow down your list by choosing only the plants you love to eat or flowers that bloom for a long time. Even if your space is a bit larger, a good way to determine how much garden you can manage is by considering how many beds you are willing to weed.

Step 6: Do the math—what can you fit based on the size of your space and the growth requirements of your plants? For example, it is often suggested to plant flower seeds with ample space in between each plant, but we find that the suggested amount of space given often just creates more freshly tilled earth for weeds to grow. We like to plant seeds closer together than suggested and thin them out as they grow, pulling the weaker ones to give the stronger, more established plants more room to grow.

Step 7: Decide if you will need to purchase starter plants or if you will buy seeds and begin growing them inside to give them a head start. If you do choose to buy seeds, flip to page 26 for our best tips on starting seeds indoors.

Step 8: Prepare the garden. Consider the soil and have mulch at the ready. For more information about this step, read our tips for feeding your soil on page 38.

Step 9: It's planting time! Have you gathered all of the tools you will need to begin? Are your homegrown seedlings ready to be sown into the earth? Mark your calendar and make it an event to be remembered, recorded, and celebrated!

Step 10: Weed, tend, observe, record—and then harvest! Harvesting is usually the part all of us dream about. It's the celebration when all of our culminating efforts reach the crescendo of botanical delight! Now that you've put in all of this time—what we commonly refer to as "sweat equity"—this phase in your gardening season again invites you in for observation. The more notes you take as you savor the bounty, the better your garden will be next year. The hands-on knowledge of this season comes in, fast and furious, and the wisdom you glean along with your kale and beans and dahlias is worth more than any internet research.

HOW TO DETERMINE WHAT WILL SUCCEED IN YOUR GARDEN

Before you decide which plants you'd like to grow, you need to determine which plants actually *can* grow in your location. Many plants can't withstand freezing temperatures, while others are cool-weather crops and will die if temperatures get too hot. To save yourself from growing plants that can't survive in your location, it's important to determine a few key factors:

1   **Your plant hardiness zone.** Find your plant hardiness zone to learn which types of plants will thrive in your specific area.

2   **Your first and last frost date.** Know your last freeze/frost date in the spring and your first freeze/frost date in the autumn to decide if you should start a seed by sowing it in the ground, starting it early indoors before the last frost, or if you should wait and purchase a transplant from your local nursery. Most importantly, these dates will also help you know when it's safe to tuck these plants into your outside garden to ensure their success.

3   **Your average growing season length.** Once you know your area's first and last frost dates, you can determine how long your expected growing season will be. Research these dates and double-check your plants' requirements. This will help you determine if it's better to start with seeds or a transplant, as well.

The USDA Plant Hardiness Zone Map can be easily accessed online at planthardiness.ars.usda.gov. Enter your address or zip code in the map's search bar to determine your location's zone.

FIND YOUR ZONE

Familiarize yourself with your area's plant hardiness zone. The United States Department of Agriculture (USDA) has published a map that divides the United States into zones based on average annual minimum temperatures. These hardiness zones determine which plants will thrive and which plants will struggle to survive in a specific zone, be it from factors like extreme heat or extreme cold. A plant's hardiness is listed on its information tag at your local nursery or in a seed catalog. You'll want to ensure that any plants you add to your garden can survive the lowest temperature listed in your area, especially perennials, trees, and shrubs, since you want them to survive in your garden for many years.

FIND YOUR FROST DATES

Knowing your first and last frost dates is important. If you start your seeds too early, cold temperatures can stall or weaken your seedlings, which makes them more susceptible to pests and disease. If you start your seeds too late for your climate, you can miss out on some precious sun and warmth, which means your plant may not reach maturity before the end of the growing season (a.k.a. your last frost date). Like most things in life, it's all about timing. Thankfully, seed packets give you great planting range suggestions, so once you know the frost date for your specific area, you can mark out the calendar in this journal and make your plant plans!

A frost date is the average date of the last frost in spring and the first frost in fall or winter. Frost occurs when air temperatures reach freezing: 32°F (0°C). However, a frost can occur even when air temperatures are just above freezing. Frost dates are different all over the country and can vary even from city to city in the same state. The dates are suggested by county or region, or even by zip code, and they are based on an average of historical climate data. When you record your area's first and last frost date, keep in mind that these are estimates and write them in pencil. Different years can be cooler or warmer, contrary to climate estimates, so keep an eye on your local forecast as you get closer to your dates and revise as necessary.

There are a few different websites you can refer to when determining your frost dates: davesgarden.com, the Old Farmer's Almanac, and the National Gardening Association. Remember to keep in mind that these dates are an average and don't take into consideration any microclimates in your garden. Also, climate change has not been taken into account when determining some frost dates.

DETERMINE THE LENGTH OF YOUR AVERAGE GROWING SEASON

Visit www.almanac.com/gardening/frostdates and enter your zip code. This website is fantastic because it also tells you how long your expected average growing season will be. If you know you need longer on those tomatoes because the seed packet's "Time to Harvest" estimate is longer than your growing season, you'll either want to start your tomato seeds inside to get a jump on your growing season or you'll want to purchase a small, established transplant from your local nursery to ensure you will be able to harvest some delicious fruit.

To see a few examples of this in action, let's look at estimates for three US cities that have unique growing climates.

Seattle, Washington (Zip Code 98125):

Zone 8b, which means plants that will thrive here can withstand low temperatures that can reach 15 to 20°F (-9.4 to -6.7°C or lower). Plants that cannot withstand 15°F should not be planted here, as they will not survive prolonged cold temperatures.

LAST SPRING FROST: March 16th

FIRST FALL FROST: November 15th

AVERAGE GROWING SEASON: 243 Days

Fargo, North Dakota (Zip Code 58102):

Zone 4a, which means plants that will thrive here can withstand low temperatures that can reach -30 to -25°F (-34.4 to -31.7°C). *Brrrr.* Plants that cannot withstand -30°F should not be planted here, as they will not survive prolonged cold temperatures.

LAST SPRING FROST: May 15th

FIRST FALL FROST: September 25th

AVERAGE GROWING SEASON: 132 Days

Zone 9a, which means plants that will thrive here can withstand low temperatures than can reach 20 to 25°F (-6.7 to -3.9°C).

While some plants will die in freezing temperatures, there are plants that require colder temperatures for a prolonged period of time in order to return the following year. A great example of these is the flowering bulb families of tulips. It's warm enough to grow tulips in one season in the Charleston area, but it doesn't usually get cold enough for a long enough time for the flowers to return.

LAST SPRING FROST: February 17th

FIRST FALL FROST: December 20th

AVERAGE GROWING SEASON: 305 Days

TRANSPLANTS VS. SEED-STARTS

Transplants

If you are new to gardening and you'd just like a great place to start with as little fuss as possible, we suggest visiting your local nursery and beginning with transplants. You can use a container on your patio in an urban location, or perhaps a small raised bed where you've noticed sunshine for 6+ hours a day.

If you want to start with a small . . .

. . .FLOWER GARDEN, we would start with these flowers:

- Pansies

- Marigolds

- Zinnias

- *Additional flowers we recommend:* Columbines, snapdragons, geraniums, salvias, coneflowers, dianthus, and cosmos

. . .HERB GARDEN, we would start with these herbs:

- Mint (Spearmint, peppermint, catnip, strawberry mint—the possibilities are endless, as are the roots of a mint plant. These plants are hardy and will spread everywhere—consider yourself warned.)

- Rosemary or sage (Both can become woody and large.)

- Chives

- *Additional herbs we recommend:* Cilantro, basil, thyme, chives, and calendula

...VEGETABLE GARDEN, we would start with these vegetables:

- Snap peas or pole beans

- Leafy greens, like spinach, kale, or lettuce

- Tomatoes

- *Additional vegetables we recommend:* zucchini or a crookneck squash (These need a lot more space, so be sure to check the requirements.)

Keep in mind, all of these suggestions can be vastly different based on your region and growing season! The best place to begin would be to visit your local gardening center and observe which plants they are offering for your area, as these should provide the most simple and successful results.

Seed-Starts

If you've done transplants and you're ready for a little more adventure, consider some of these quick and reliable easy-to-germinate seeds. We've included step-by-step instructions for starting seeds on page 26!

Flowers

You can germinate flower seeds, although it is always easiest to do flowers as transplants! They just take longer to germinate (sometimes 2-3 weeks before you even get a sprout!). Personally, we prefer transplanted flowers every year as annuals, as well as a few garden beds of perennial bulbs and tubers (more on these on the following page).

- Calendulas or marigolds
- Pincushion flowers
- Cosmos
- Stock
- Zinnias

Herbs

- Sage
- Cilantro
- Chives
- Borage

Vegetables

- Snap peas
- Lettuce
- Radishes
- Fennel
- Arugula (a.k.a. rocket)

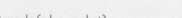

Bulbs, Corms, Tubers, and Rhizomes

The beauty of these plants is not just in their tremendous blossoms, but (for most climates) it's also in their perennial return every year. It is a delight to do so little yet be rewarded with so much year after year! We encourage you to research these incredible plants with underground food storage organs, as we enjoy so many of them in our garden. A few of our favorites are:

- Tulips (bulbs)
- Gladioluses (corms)
- Dahlias (tubers)
- Bearded irises (rhizomes)

We could fill an entire garden journal on just bearded irises alone, but for efficiency, we invite you to check out the Additional Resources section on page 184 to learn about some companies that have already gathered and shared their bountiful knowledge with us all.

Don't judge each day by the harvest you reap but by the seeds that you plant.

—ROBERT LOUIS STEVENSON

Plant lives are similar to people: They go through distinct stages with different needs during growth periods. It's helpful to know the names of these plant stages and their needs so you can address them as their caretaker:

1   <u>Seed</u>:

Out of the packet and into your hand! Seed packets come with a wealth of information, and taking a moment to read about your plant's needs now will set you up for success in the future. Does your plant prefer to be directly seeded into the earth? Check your last frost date and mark your calendar for a planting day. Some seeds can just as easily be planted into the earth as in a seed tray, so if you have a chance to give your plants a head start inside, it's always nice. Your seed packet will let you know how much sun is needed for a successful growing season, as well.

2   <u>Seedling</u>:

A result of the germination process, this is also known as a sprout! Roots begin to form during this stage, as well as stems and early leaves. Well-balanced nutrients of NPK help this growth, and specially formulated seed starting soil mixes give them a jump start. (See page 39 for info on the nutrients NPK.)

3   <u>Vegetative</u>:

This stage in your plant's life is all about growing strong and healthy stems and leaves, which are gathering nutrients needed for flowering. Nitrogen is the most important nutrient at this stage. The transplants you purchase from your local nursery are usually at this stage, but this is also when you would transplant the seeds you began inside to their outside spots.

4 Budding:

Phosphorus is the most essential nutrient during this phase, which helps plants put energy into their reproduction. Most plants will get everything they need from the soil; however, it's helpful to read plant labels and research your specific plant needs to see if fertilizer would be helpful.

5 Flowering:

Potassium is your macronutrient most desired now, which helps your plant develop full, healthy blooms and fruit. This is when pollination is happening, thanks to the birds and the bees and the butterflies!

6 Ripening:

As your plant reaches full maturity, water is needed now. Pollinated flowers ripen with fruit, which contains the seeds of new baby plants to come. Carefully observing when fruit needs to be plucked, or when the plant may need extra support, is helpful as well.

HOW TO START SEEDS INDOORS

There is always something to do in the garden, even if it's merely dreaming of the next season and what you would like to grow!

One gardening task that you can begin while the earth is still cold outside is starting seeds—indoors! Growing seeds indoors gives you a head start on the season, and by the time the earth is warmed and ready to cultivate, you will have small transplants to add to your garden beds. Growing from hand-selected seeds also allows you to fill your garden with plants that your local nursery may not carry, giving you a chance to grow things that excite you. I love seeking out heirloom flower varietals to grow in my garden and then use in bouquets and as painting inspiration. Planting heirloom seeds encourages biodiversity and ensures rich heritage and stories will continue to be shared.

Of course, there are more advanced and involved ways to really prolong the growing season wherever you are, and these methods involve a whole range of tools, from grow lights to greenhouses and cold frames to frost cloths. Check out the Additional Resources section (page 184) if you're ready to increase your harvest or push your garden for more adventures.

For now, however, we will cover the basic steps for beginning seeds indoors.

Materials Needed:

- Seeds

- Seed-starting mix

- Seed tray flats and/or pots (new or upcycled)

- Leakproof trays to catch the water beneath the seed trays

- Plant tags

- Clear acrylic dome lids to hold in moisture and heat

- Heat mat(s)
- Lights

You do not need anything over-the-top fancy to start seeds, like grow lights, heating pads, a greenhouse, etc. These will make the process easier, sure, but they are not necessary. Find a sunny window* where you get the most light, and make sure you have drip trays to catch excess water.

*A south-facing window is ideal, but if you notice that your window doesn't get 6-8 hours of light, you may want to consider a grow light to increase your success!

1   **PREPARE THE SEED-STARTING CONTAINERS.** These can be anything from seed trays, seedling cups, small terra-cotta pots, or even old egg cartons. You want good drainage when starting seeds, because most seeds prefer the soil to stay wet (but not flooded). Ideally, you will want to use seed trays because they have shallow wells and are intended for this purpose. You also won't have to use as much soil, and trays usually come with lids to help keep in the warmth as they germinate. Another benefit is that you can use seed trays again and again!

2   **FILL THE CONTAINERS WITH SEED-STARTING SOIL.** Seed-starting soil mixes are specially created to have all of the nutrients needed to start your seeds off right.

3   **FOLLOW THE SEED PACKET INSTRUCTIONS** for how deep to plant your seeds. Generally, it is advised that you sow seeds at a depth two times the width of a seed. You can use plant markers to remind yourself which seed is which.

4   **CREATE YOUR OWN LITTLE GREENHOUSE** by covering your seeds with a clear plastic lid. A clear plastic bag will work too!

5   **PLACE YOUR SEEDS SOMEWHERE WARM THAT GETS NAT-
    URAL LIGHT**—a south-facing window is best if you have it! Try
    to avoid hot, direct sun, as this can scorch the seedlings. Seed
    packets will usually suggest ideal soil temperatures for germina-
    tion, and you can place your seedling tray on a heat mat if you
    want to invest in this extra tool. But you will generally see the
    greatest success if your seedlings are at a room temperature of
    68–78°F. Grow lights can be employed for the darker northern
    climates or any indoor growing areas that do not get enough natu-
    ral light. Once the seed sprouts, the best growing temperature for
    the seedling is around 10°F cooler than the optimum germination
    temperature. You don't want your seedlings to dry out from too
    much heat once they have germinated.

6   **KEEP THE SOIL MOIST!** Seeds need warmth and light to grow,
    but they also need consistent moisture. You do not want your
    seeds' soil to dry out! Commercially available seed-starter con-
    tainers come with lids to help keep moisture in, but also having a
    water-catching tray beneath your seed-starting containers allows
    you to keep the soil moist. After you sow your seeds, use a water-
    ing can to add water to the water-catching tray beneath. You can
    mist your seeds from the top, but most seeds prefer to be watered
    from the bottom.

7   **THIN YOUR SPROUTED SEEDS** so that the strongest can flour-
    ish. Thinning each plant during the seedling/vegetative state while
    they are still in their seed containers saves you time later, and can
    provide a delicious dish of microgreens to munch on now.

8   **PLANT YOUR "STARTS,"** a.k.a. "transplants," into your garden
    once the earth has warmed and you've noted the time from the
    last frost. Check your seed packet for spacing suggestions as well,
    and be aware that if you plant transplants too closely, you may
    have to thin some later.

A few helpful hints on how to select seeds:

- Be aware of your first and last frost dates, hardiness zone, and potential growing season time. Check out page 16 to learn more about these before you begin.

- Order catalogs from seed companies (check out the Additional Resources section on page 184 for some of our favorite seed companies), and then curl up with a warm cup of tea and a pencil and get ready to dog-ear your favorite pages. Seed catalogs are free and can be requested on the company's website. A good seed catalog is filled with beautiful photos of the varieties you can grow, along with seed history, growing resources, and even suggested recipes to use in your kitchen once you've got your harvested fruits and vegetables. So inspiring!

- Know your garden. How much light does your space have to offer? What is the condition of your soil? You may want to grow over-the-top gigantic watermelons, but if you aren't in the right area for it, you will only be disappointed.

- Read reviews and ensure that the company you are ordering from has consistently great germination rates. Some seeds will sprout, and others will not—this happens to everyone. You would ideally like a 90% germination rate for your seeds, and good companies will share theirs.

A Note from Sarah

As a child, my grandfather had the most magical garden. I have the fondest memories of playing hide-and-seek with my cousins amongst the rows of giant sunflowers. When he passed, my aunt gave me the gift of a packet of seeds from these beloved flowers. The first year I started them, I wondered if they would be as magical as I remembered;

nostalgia often sweetens things, and gazing up at sky-high sunflowers as a child means they might not be quite as majestic for an adult. Oh, how wrong I was. These seeds were less than a quarter of an inch long, and within a few weeks, their stalks were so thick I couldn't wrap my hand around them. Every year we plant a small forest of sunflowers from my grandfather's flower seeds, and every year I give baby sunflower starts to every neighbor who would like one (or five). These bold yellow giants rocket to the sky and loom large over any fence, with large faces that follow the path of the sun. Neighborhood walks feel like an extra special joy during late summer, as we see the granddaughters and great-granddaughters of the original seeds up and down our street, peering around houses and in the gardens of even the most timid gardener.

Planting is a community builder, and there is often a story to tell about all the different plants in your garden. Sharing the seeds from my grandfather's sunflowers has been a great encourager, prompting so many wonderful conversations with neighbors, whom we now call friends. I hope you find that beginning a garden is one of the best ways to make new friends—whether it's online or right in your own backyard. If you do decide to trade or share seeds with neighbors or friends, I highly recommend borage, sunflower, and foxglove* seeds, as well as divided bulbs of lilies and bearded irises.

*Beware the foxglove . . . They are stunning but VERY poisonous for humans and furry friends alike. Never plant them near edibles.

While it is fun to plant an array of colorful flowers and unique vegetables, it is helpful to understand your specific region and consider the beneficial impacts of a native plant. According to USDA.gov, "Native plants are the indigenous terrestrial and aquatic species that have evolved and occur naturally in a particular region, ecosystem, and habitat." Planting native plants into your garden increases your green thumb* success rate for all of the reasons below:

- They are naturally healthier and stronger, which is always encouraging as a gardener.

- They are lower maintenance to care for, as their needs are more naturally met in your environment.

- They are important for your region and support the natural fauna that you as a gardener want in your space by providing nectar for pollinators (think hummingbirds, native bees, and butterflies).

- They reduce energy consumption and pollution.

- They reduce the need for pesticides, since they thrive in your natural conditions already.

- They are more naturally adapted to local growing conditions and often require fewer inputs (fertilizer, water, etc.) for successful establishment in your garden.

While we still love to grow different types of flowers, herbs, and vegetables, it's worth researching your area's native plants, because growing these can help your garden thrive!

Have you heard the term "green thumb"? It's a way to say someone has a natural talent for growing plants, and it is often alluded to with an almost mystical aura surrounding it, with a hushed whisper of awe. However, it's not a magical gift one is born with and knows intrinsically; it is a cultivated and hard-won skill set that is worthy of your pursuit.

COMMON GARDENING TERMS

If you're a first-time gardener, you may feel overwhelmed by the sheer amount of information available in books, articles, and social media. (We've been gardening for more than fifteen years, and we're *still* learning about new gardening techniques!) Because this can often be overwhelming to new gardeners, we've highlighted the main topics and definitions you're likely to come across as you dive into the world of gardening.

Each of the following topics has been researched extensively by the gardening community, and you could spend days—and yes, even years—familiarizing yourself with the encyclopedic level of knowledge that has been shared about these topics in books, journals, videos, articles, and online forums. In this journal, we provide brief definitions and a few best practices for each. Should you find your fascination with gardening growing, we encourage you to dive deep into the topics that resonate with you most.

Perennials, Annuals, and Biennials

Your growing season depends on where you live, the temperature, and the amount of sun you receive on your little plot of land in this great big wide world of ours. Plants will grow in your area based on these factors, and you can consider the days that your plants are in the ground as your general "growing season." As you might imagine, some regions have longer growing seasons than others, and where a plant is grown will determine how long its life is.

ANNUAL is a term that refers to plants that complete their entire life cycle in one *annual* growing season. Annuals germinate, leaf, flower, produce seeds, and die within the course of a year. If you want to grow them again, you'll need to replant new plants in your garden the following year. Annuals are often listed as "tender" with little or no cold tolerance, or "half-hardy" and "hardy" with a decent amount of tolerance to the cold. Annual plants offer a chance to try something exciting and new in your garden—or a chance to invite your favorites back every year as you get better and better at germinating seeds.

Typically, if a plant is a perennial but it's too delicate to handle winter temperatures, you can grow it as an annual. Conversely, hardy annuals in temperate climate zones can be grown as perennials!

PERENNIAL is a term used for plants that come back year after year, without replanting in a new growing season. Perennials are plants that, after their growing season, will pull all of their energy back into their structure and store up their resources for the next growing season, often appearing dead (a.k.a. dormant) during the cold winter weather. Like annuals, perennials are also often listed as tender, half-hardy, and hardy. Dahlias can be considered tender perennials and depending on the zone, can either be left in the ground to bloom again for the next year or, if your zone's winters are just too cold, will need to be dug up and stored inside if you want them to survive the winter. Half-hardy perennials can withstand cold to a point, whereas hardy perennials—like fennel and sage—can be left alone and depended upon to keep on coming back year after year. Perennials come in summer and winter varieties. The best planting time for perennials varies by your specific zone, but generally you will plant winter perennials in early autumn and summer perennials in the early spring. This gives the plants time to establish their root systems before the weather gets too warm or too cold.

BIENNIAL is a term used for plants that complete their life cycle over *two* growing seasons. Biennial plants—like foxgloves, for example—germinate during the autumn or spring months and produce roots, a stem, and leaves in their first year, storing up energy before going dormant. The following second year, they produce flowers, fruit, and seeds. They are classified as tender, half-hardy, and hardy just like annuals and perennials.

Pruning

Also referred to as trimming, cutting, chopping, snipping, lopping . . . we could go on. The intention of pruning in a garden is to remove dead or dying debris, to aesthetically shape or manicure, and to promote healthy growth on your plant. Some plants should be pruned, while others should not, and each plant has certain preferences for WHEN it should be pruned and when it should NOT be pruned. For example, if a camellia bush is pruned in the fall, you will accidentally remove all of its winter blooms. But if you give it a late spring pruning after it has flowered, you will stimulate new growth and allow for the lower branches to receive more sunlight. By researching the specific plant you are tending to, you can find all of its pruning preferences and ensure its success.

Mulching

In its simplest form, *mulch is any material that covers the soil's surface.* Mulching happens automatically in nature; think of fallen leaves and plant debris in a forest. In a self-tended garden, we can add different types of mulch to get the same effect that happens organically in nature. Why mulch? Mulch helps to increase soil moisture, reduce weed growth, moderate soil temperature, improve the harvest quality, and protect the soil and your plants—while also feeding the soil. Your soil is a living microorganism that needs replenishment and intentional care and by mulching, you are tending it well. Depending on where you live, you can use the most natural resource available to mulch your garden. For example, in Washington, wood chips are readily available; in South Carolina, most gardeners mulch with pine straw.

Weeding

A good way to determine how much garden you can manage is by considering how many beds you are willing to weed. Weeds are in direct competition with your plants for the finite resources in the soil—and for space. Weeds can block sunlight, too. One of the most necessary and regular chores of the garden, it was often given to both of us as a "punishment" when we were kids, much like the annual raking of fall leaves. However, now that we've grown up and have a garden of our own, we both have come to see it as a cathartic way to tend and regularly observe what's happening in the garden. New plants and buds emerge daily in the spring, and what better way to be familiar with the most recent news of the earth than to be digging around, tending the beds yourself? By removing unwanted "volunteers" from your well-cultivated plot, you ensure weeds (for example, dandelions) don't become established and steal all of the nutrients from your intentionally planted flowers or vegetables. A little weeding every day during spring, summer, and fall is a necessary chore, but you can make it fun with headphones or as a family activity (we pay my kids for full buckets!). You can hoe or kneel and pick, but always meander and be on the constant lookout for rogue weeds determined to leech delicious nutrients from your intentionally planted garden. This is an "always" task for the gardener, and unless the earth is buried in feet of snow, there is always a weed to find. Granted, the weeds are *under* the snow as well; we just can't see them yet.

Supports

Stakes, bamboo canes, tomato cages, trellises, fences, and hoops! For windy climates or tall and top-heavy plants (especially when they begin to reach harvest time and become laden with fruit), it can be helpful to provide them with a little support. We use twine or long green twist ties to tie up our tall bearded iris stalks so the weight of their blooms doesn't snap their stems, and the same can be done for any plants that just need a little extra help. Beautiful gardens often include height! Adding that extra dimension to your growing plans not only gives your plants more space to run (up, up to the sun!) but also increases the visual delight of your garden scape. Make note of where you would like to add a trellis or perhaps a handmade arch from a neighbor's discarded fig tree branches, as height will cast a shadow on any plants behind it. Stake your plants before they need it; I have had a bearded iris stem flop over from a good rain and snap before I could help. Small fences can act as relieving windbreaks for a more rugged climate and provide a bit of shade from the intense summer sun.

Deadheading

This is the process of pinching or removing aging blooms from the plant to promote new growth and re-flowering. A great example of a flower that rewards you as a faithful deadheading gardener is a pansy; the more you pinch off, the more blooms you get! Sometimes the pansy will overwinter in Seattle and parade around the container garden like a perennial, but most of the time in the Pacific Northwest, it's an annual. However, I don't mind investing in lots of frilly pansy plants every spring because they are so prolific! There are many varietals that are edible as well as beautiful, so these unique little flowers grace my table in more than just bouquets throughout the spring, summer, and fall. I freeze their petals in ice cubes and add them to beverages as beautiful garnishes, and I top cakes and salads with them for party guests. Deadheading, like weeding, keeps you in daily contact with your garden beds and can be incredibly relaxing, rewarding, and meditative.

Thinning

This is a practice you will use when working with seedlings, whether it's for the seed trays you start inside or the beds you plant outside in your garden. Thinning seedlings means removing some of the weaker ones that were perhaps planted too closely together so that only the best and strongest ones are left to thrive. If you choose to plant a crop of greens, you can thin out the plants when they are young to help the others grow, then make yourself a little salad of microgreens. Thinning gives full-grown plants the space they will need to grow to their fullest potential.

Feeding

There are two things you are constantly feeding as a gardener: your plants and also your soil. As plants grow, they use the nutrients from your soil, which eventually needs to be replenished.

Some plants are referred to as "heavy-feeders," which means they need more nutrients to flourish. They receive these nutrients both from the soil they are growing in and fertilizer (a.k.a. plant food) supplemented by the gardener. Properly fed plants establish stronger, more efficient roots; don't take as much from the soil (and other nearby plants); and give you a better harvest. Different plants have different feeding needs, both in the composition of what they require, when they want it, and where they like it (for example, on their leaves or roots).

- Plants need nutrients to grow healthy stems, leaves, flowers, and fruit.

- The major nutrients needed are nitrogen, phosphorus, and potassium, often referred to as NPK.

- Fertilizer bags will refer to the percentages of these three macronutrients on their labels. The first number is for nitrogen (N), the second for phosphorous (P), and the third for potassium (K). For example, general use fertilizers will often have an NPK ratio of 10-10-10 or 20-20-20.

- Fertilizers are tailored to specific plants or soil conditions. For example, I love growing bearded irises, and they are heavy feeders. They prefer a low-nitrogen fertilizer, such as a 5-10-10. Instructions on the fertilizer help you to learn where to apply the fertilizer to amend the soil around the plant to give you long-lasting, big, healthy blooms.

You can amend your soil with fertilizers or with compost (so many lengthy and fascinating books can be found on this subject!). But how do you know what your soil needs? Before you panic and start to get lost in the proverbial compost weeds, pause. Most likely, if you're starting with fresh soil in a container or raised bed every year, you may not have to amend your soil much—if at all—since the new soil comes rich in these macronutrients.

Composting

If you're a returning gardener or you're ready to take your gardening to the next level, researching compost containers and natural composting methods, as well as soil test kits and fertilizers, would be a helpful next step. Because yes, you actually can and do want to feed your soil. This is where crop rotation comes in, and all of the incredible science behind companion planting, as well.

Here are just a few natural suggestions for what you can compost to help feed your soil:

- Grass clippings (rich in nitrogen)
- Weeds
- Kitchen scraps
- Manure
- Tree leaves
- Coffee grounds
- Eggshells
- Banana peels

Learning to invest in your soil by continuing to compost in your home garden not only feeds your garden, but it helps recycle household kitchen waste. For example, we often gather other yard scraps—like grass clippings and old Halloween pumpkins—to add to our compost bins. We also regularly stop by the local coffee shops to pick up their spent coffee grounds, which help add nutrient-rich nitrogen to the compost bins.

Watering

This is another necessary step in your garden, especially on the warm days of summer. Most plants prefer being watered at the base of their structure, right where the plant comes out of the earth. Delivering the water right to the source—the roots—saves your plant from leaf fungus, and you will lose less water to evaporation in the air. You may want to use a watering can for small container gardens, or perhaps consider a watering nozzle and/or watering wand from your local hardware or nursery. The wand and nozzle connect to your hose so you can alter the spray, as well as reach farther. We like to use the soaking setting, right at the roots. It's gentle but steady and doesn't overwhelm young plants or erode the soil away from tender roots like a regular hose spray. Another alternative, should you have a larger garden or you know you won't remember to water regularly, is a soaker hose. Unlike regular hoses, a soaker hose is porous, and when wound around a garden bed and staked down for the season, it will drip water gently into your garden for as long as you'd like. You can hook this up to a timer if you want to get fancy, and it offers great peace of mind knowing your plants are being regularly watered—one less thing for you to think about! To water efficiently in your garden, start with 30 minutes twice a week and adjust as needed based on the weather (no rain means more watering needed!). Notice how your plants are responding to the amount of water they receive and continue to adjust accordingly.

Cover Crops

"Cover crops" is a term often heard in the gardening world, and it has everything to do with your soil health. If you are just beginning to garden and bringing in new soil for your beds, the nutrients from your soil will be enough to grow flourishing plants. But once your soil is on its second growing season, you are going to need to replenish it with nutrients so it can keep on giving. Plants use up the nutrients in the soil to grow big and strong, and while replenishing with organic compost and fertilizers in the spring is helpful, an additional method for improving your soil health that is inexpensive, built into the growth cycle, and fantastic for suppressing early spring weeds is planting cover crops.

Cover crops are plants (for example, grains, grasses, or legumes) that grow during fall and winter. You can plan on cutting, mowing, tilling, and working them directly into the earth in the spring.

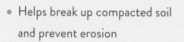

- Helps break up compacted soil and prevent erosion

- Helps aerate soil with roots that penetrate and helps loosen heavy clumps, increasing air and water flow

- When you till (or break down) cover crops into your soil, the plants add organic matter, increasing better soil structure and fertility

- Legume cover crops (for example, clover, peas, etc.) add nitrogen to the soil by transferring the nitrogen from the atmosphere and putting it back into the ground. They can also contain nitrogen and other mineral nutrients that they deposit into the soil that the winter rains usually wash away.

Crop Rotation

Rotating where you plant specific vegetables or flowers every year is a wonderful way to mix it up in your home garden, but this practice also has lots of practical purposes beyond aesthetic pleasure. By adjusting the location of where you plant every year, you can reduce insect and pest damage (they like to return to the same spot to feed, and if their favorite dinner from last year isn't in the same spot, they move on); limit the amount of diseases that afflict your vegetables; and give you a chance to manage your soil's nutrient levels, which can help supplement your earth with nutrients for a surge in harvest for the following year.

"Direct Sow" vs. "Seed-Start" vs. "Transplant"

Direct sowing involves putting the seed, as the name implies, directly into the earth of your garden. Seed starting is when you begin your plants indoors (or in a greenhouse), giving them a head start while the earth outside may still be frosty and inhospitable. (For step-by-step instructions on how to start plants from seeds, turn to page 26.) You would then transplant these "starts" into the garden once they have reached a more mature stage and the dirt is warm enough. (More information about the plant stage cycle can be found on page 24.) There needs to be enough light for the seedlings to thrive, and timing is important to note. A transplant can come from your own seed-starts or from a local plant nursery (and sometimes a helpful hardware store). The plants are already at a mature age, ready to be directly planted into your garden. Deciding whether to direct sow, start your seeds indoors, or transplant directly into the garden comes down to the type of plant you're growing and its requirements based on your hardiness zone. Many seed packets will suggest a recommended method based on the plant's needs, but you can always do a quick search to determine what's best for you.

Planting by the Moon

Before modern science and generations of farming practices were finally captured and shared with the masses, there was the tradition of planting by the moon. Humans' lives revolved around the seasons, and the celestial bodies governed days and nights of planting traditions. Scientifically, we understand more about the moon's gravitational force and its effects on us Earth dwellers. If you think of the ocean tides, and how the moon pulls water upward, you can begin to see how, as the theory goes, the new and full moons are better times to plant seeds because there is more moisture in the top sowing layers of soil. If this interests you, there is fascinating evidence to study online about how the different moon phases affect different types of plants, as well as biodynamic gardening tips.

Companion Planting

Companion planting is a fabulous way to maximize space in your garden while also building a thriving and natural ecosystem—right in your own little garden plot. Throughout the history of planting, shared knowledge has taught many a serious farmer and dabbler gardener alike that some plants naturally thrive when planted next to one another. When you plant mint among your lettuce, it helps to keep away the slugs that feed on lettuce leaves. Cilantro pairs well with tomatoes, chilies, and onions, and marigolds can help repel aphids, which are a com-

mon pest of lettuce and cucumbers. While some plants do not do as well next to one another and actually will compete for space and nutrients (for example, beans and onions or tomatoes and corn), there is a wealth of knowledge to be gleaned from mutually beneficial relationships. One of our favorite companion plant relationships widely used by Native American farming societies is the trio of corn, pole beans, and squash, commonly known as the "Three Sisters." Here's how it works: the pole beans use the corn stalks as support to grow, while at the same time stabilizing the corn with their strong tendrils. The beans also help restore nitrogen to the soil for future crops. Because squash sprawls as it grows, it keeps weeds down, shades the soil, and helps prevent moisture from evaporating from the surface.

Succession Planting

This approach is the best way to continue to enjoy fresh herbs and vegetables all season long. Plant the first round of seeds in the first workable soil of the season or start a tray of seedlings indoors. After these seeds have sprouted and are established in your garden, usually about 3–4 weeks later, plant another round of seeds. As the first round is harvested and enjoyed, your second round will be close on its heels. And you can repeat this planting cycle throughout the growing season to ensure you always have a fresh and continuous supply. When you're making plans for succession gardening, be sure to check the seed's "time to harvest" estimate and mark your calendar with likely dates.

Square Foot Gardening

Coined by Mel Bartholomew, square foot gardening (or SFG) is a fun and approachable way to lay out your garden beds. It's the practice of dividing your growing area into small, square sections, filling each section with different plants. For example, a raised garden bed that is 3 feet by 3 feet would have 9 square feet, so you could plant a different type of lettuce in each square! Or you could add some variety, and based on each plant's needs, you could plant one extra-large plant in one square, two large plants in one square, four medium plants in one square, etc. The goal of this type of gardening is to maximize space and provide a logical way to lay out your garden beyond the traditional row planting, while creating a dense and varied garden plot.

Container Gardening

If your space is limited, narrow down your "must-grow" list by choosing only the plants you love to eat or flowers that bloom for a long time. Select a large container with drainage, and if you are hoping to add some root vegetables to your container garden (yes, you can!), just make sure it's deeper than 18 inches, so you give those carrots room to stretch. Another common problem of gardening in a smaller space is that you are often limited in how much sun exposure you may have. There are some plants that only need around 4 hours of sun and are great for containers: lettuce, Swiss chard, mustards, and herbs. Borage, mint, geraniums, begonias, and pansies are also some of my favorites for containers. You can always add a trellis of vertical supports and grow more—just up! And don't forget to water!

Bolting

Most fruits and vegetables flower in order to reproduce, which we expect as gardeners, but in the vegetable garden it can be frustrating when a plant "goes to seed" or "bolts" before we would like. Bolting describes an edible, frost-tolerant plant like lettuce, cilantro, or other greens quickly going to seed. When this happens, the quality of the produce goes down. For example, you eat romaine lettuce for its leaves, but if it bolts, the plant puts all of its energy into creating seeds, leaving the leaves lacking in that desired delicious flavor. Certain varieties of plants have been bred to be more bolt-resistant and we suggest looking for these to sow into your garden. Any time there is a drastic change in temperature—like a swing in spring-time temperatures towards a more drought-like summer climate—the plant stresses out a bit and decides it needs to use its resources to make flowers and then seeds, rather than staying in that delicious, harvestable state we desire. To avoid bolting, besides investing in bolt-resistant varietals, we suggest watering consistently, paying attention to your sunlight, and sowing plants where they may get a bit of a rest in the afternoon shade. But most importantly, it's mainly about when you plant them. For example, starting a lettuce crop in the heat of the summer isn't going to give the plant time to produce a good or lengthy crop. By sticking to the planting season that your varietal

suggests (check the plant seed packet and calculate those frost dates based on how many days it takes the plant to reach maturity), you'll set yourself up for the most success.

Harvesting

How do you know when it's time? Harvesting is the process of gathering a crop when it's reached its peak flavor, and every plant is different, of course. Harvesting is the most time-sensitive activity in your garden, right behind watering and weeding, but it is by far the most fulfilling.

Plants like tomatoes or cucumbers are pretty self-explanatory. Most vegetables are ready to harvest when they reach a usable size. And a taste test is always a wonderful way to check in with your vegetables. However, root vegetables like carrots are underground . . . so how do you know? The radish is another great example. Radishes are relatively quick to harvest, and if you let them go too long, the radish itself becomes a fibrous, inedible root that gives all of its nutrients to flowers and then seeds.

There are no exact rules to follow for the perfect time to harvest, and great flavor isn't a simple matter of size or color. However, there are a few notes you can make as you learn about your plants that will help you. Approximate harvest dates can be noted in this journal when you sow your seeds (use the Plant Logs chart starting on page 64 to keep track). Pay attention, check the plant seed packet to calculate the best sowing dates based on your last frost, and then make note of how many days it will take the plant to reach maturity.

A daily garden walk around the harvest time you've noted in your journal is quite fruitful (literally) and always an adventure. Take a stroll with a basket over your arm, visit each plant in your care, lift its leaves, peer at its stalk, assess its fruit— just take time to observe your plants. You will begin to speak their language in no time at all.

Pests and Diseases

SLUGS AND SNAILS: Rain is a delight to a gardener, most of the time, as it checks off the chore of watering the garden. However, spring rains often bring a not-so-desired result as well: pests. Rain draws out the slugs and snails, and their slimy, iridescent trails can often be followed right to your most prized plants. These types of pests are most active at night or on colder, cloudy days. The best solution to these common pests is *prevention*. By tidying your garden and removing weeds, leaves, or surrounding debris, you are removing slugs' and snails' favorite places to hide and lay eggs.

There are other ways to deter these pests as well, including pet-friendly snail bait and exclusion barriers such as cracked filbert shells, plant cloches, and collars. There's an old wives' tale that using copper as a repellant may do the trick, so a row of protective pennies, being coated in copper, could help repel these bugs. Protecting your plants from pests is important—not just aesthetically, as the snails do a gnawing number to your fresh, new leaves—but because their gnawing diminishes photosynthetic activity and creates wounds that make the plants more susceptible to attracting other pests and disease. There are many plant-, kid-, and animal-friendly pesticide-free products that help pests stay out of your garden. Sluggo® is our go-to for the early spring munchers and is truly organic, with its active ingredient being phosphate.

NEIGHBORHOOD CATS: You wouldn't necessarily think of these beautiful feline friends as pests, and they are fabulous at keeping other obnoxious creatures out of your garden (think rats), but they do have a tendency to use freshly tilled garden beds as litter-box havens. And you do not want to eat anything raw in your garden—or even spend time gardening—if you are pregnant, if there's a chance of cats using your garden beds for their potty time. But to prevent neighbor cats, feral or tame, from pooping in your pristine beds, we suggest pet-friendly chicken wire, bamboo skewers (pointy side up), or heavy mulches. These are friendly ways of deterring them from getting a bit too comfortable and using your freshly turned bed as a litter box.

A FEW FINAL THOUGHTS

Like most things in life, gardening is all about good timing. As with any new or creative pursuit, your beginning mindset matters. Hope and courage and a little flutter of excitement to begin should be balanced with a healthy mindset and realistic goals and expectations.

START SMALL. You do not need to grow every flower, fruit, and vegetable on your dream bucket list this season, and you will be more successful—and learn more—if you start small. Ambition is wondrous, but we learn the best bit by bit. Select a few flowers or a few herbs to begin your first year and LEARN from all of the trial and error to come.

Gardens can quickly become a lot to manage in the harvesting season, which is an absolute delight and success—and it's obviously a gardener's goal. However, keep the "start small" idea in mind; remember that you do not need to plant an entire farm's worth of zucchini your first season. Trust me: We did that and after baking fourteen loaves of zucchini bread and processing enough frozen zucchini noodles to require an extra garage freezer, we listened to our neighbors (who were also politely refusing more zucchini) and decided to only plant what we could eat.

KEEP UP THAT CURIOSITY. Become a regular at your local nursery. Or stop peeping through your neighbor's fence and bring them some cookies and ask them about their plants. Every green thumb is eager to share. Bring a notepad along (or perhaps this journal) with those friendly neighbor cookies to share and soak in all of that hard-won knowledge: What is growing well here in our micro-climate? What is that plant called? Did you start that plant from seed? When did you start them? Can you save me some of those foxgloves seeds for next season? Wait, what is a biennial? You will learn something new every time, every season. The community you build as you practice being a lifelong learner will only enrich your entire experience.

OBSERVE, RECORD, ADJUST. And that's what these pages are for: all of your observations, hard-won lessons, and tips from generations of others who have gone before us. Turn the word "failure'" on its head and reassign the thought: Instead of saying "I failed at tomatoes," say "I learned that next time, tomatoes need . . ." Gardening is a never-ending experiment, and making mistakes may teach you more than having nothing but successes.

Part Two

PLAN YOUR GARDEN

SUN TRACKER

As you plan your garden and dream up which plants you'd love to grow, it's important to know how much sun your garden receives throughout the day. Because sunlight levels in a particular area of your yard can change each season, we recommend completing this chart twice: once in the spring and once in midsummer.

Spring

LOCATION	6:00 AM	7:00 AM	8:00 AM	9:00 AM	10:00 AM	11:00 AM	12:00 PM
Front Flower Bed	Shade	Shade	Shade	Shade	Partial Sun	Partial Sun	Full Sun

Midsummer

LOCATION	6:00 AM	7:00 AM	8:00 AM	9:00 AM	10:00 AM	11:00 AM	12:00 PM

1:00 PM	2:00 PM	3:00 PM	4:00 PM	5:00 PM	6:00 PM	7:00 PM	8:00 PM	9:00 PM
Full Sun	Full Sun	Full Sun	Full Sun	Full Sun	Partial Sun	Shade	Shade	Shade

1:00 PM	2:00 PM	3:00 PM	4:00 PM	5:00 PM	6:00 PM	7:00 PM	8:00 PM	9:00 PM

GARDEN PLANNING GRIDS

Use these pages to sketch out your dream garden! You could draw your garden beds to scale, filling in each area with the plants you hope to grow. Or, you could doodle beautiful flowers to help inspire the mood you want to create in your garden. Use these pages however you need and make them your own!

SEASONAL CHORES TRACKER

No matter the season, there are always garden chores to be done to ensure your garden is maintained throughout the year! Check out our annual list, then flip the page to create your own.

FALL

- ○ Maintain soil
- ○ Collect final harvest
- ○ Plant winter crops
- ○ Pull weeds
- ○ Trim back each plant
- ○ Rake the yard & store leaves as brown source for compost
- ○ Remove dead plants or perennials that are done for the year
- ○ Move non-hardy plants indoors before the first frost
- ○ Shut off outdoor faucets
- ○ Clean & store any maintenance tools, like garden hoses & unused flower pots
- ○ Save available seeds for next year's harvest
- ○ Request seed catalogs

WINTER

- ○ Maintain soil
- ○ Plan garden for next year
- ○ Save containers for seed starting, like egg cartons and clean yogurt containers
- ○ Start stocking up on seeds
- ○ Start seedlings indoors (if applicable)
- ○ Sharpen garden tools
- ○ Replace or repair any damaged garden tools and containers

SPRING

- Check soil pH and make amendments
- Mulch beds
- Prune trees and bushes that flower in the spring
- Start late-season seedlings
- Check garden hoses for any leaks and repair if needed

SUMMER

- Tie up leggy/tall plants to supports (tomatoes, beans, and flowers may need extra support)
- Regularly weed garden beds
- Fertilize heavy-feeder plants, like tomatoes
- Harvest fruits, vegetables, and herbs as they ripen
- Walk around other gardens in your area, whether it's a local park, shopping center, or neighbors' gardens. This can inspire you for next year's planning and you can learn a lot about what grows well where you live based on what others are having success with.

Your Seasonal Chores Tracker

FALL

○ _____
○ _____
○ _____
○ _____
○ _____
○ _____
○ _____
○ _____

WINTER

○ _____
○ _____
○ _____
○ _____
○ _____
○ _____
○ _____
○ _____

SPRING

○ _____
○ _____
○ _____
○ _____
○ _____
○ _____
○ _____
○ _____

SUMMER

○ _____
○ _____
○ _____
○ _____
○ _____
○ _____
○ _____
○ _____

Part Three

PLANT LOGS

PLANT NAME (and varietal)	SOURCE	PLANTING LOCATION	ANNUAL OR PERENNIAL	WHEN TO START SEEDS INSIDE	DAYS TO GERMINATION
Snap Peas (Sugar Daddy Snap)	Seed Company	Raised garden bed in front garden	Annual	N/A; direct sow into garden	5–10 days

LIGHT NEEDS	SPACE REQUIREMENTS	PLANTING DATE	HARVESTING DATE	NOTES
Partial sun	Space 2 feet apart	March 22	May 24	- These do better in the colder spring before too much summer heat - Need support/trellising

PLANT NAME (and varietal)	SOURCE	PLANTING LOCATION	ANNUAL OR PERENNIAL	WHEN TO START SEEDS INSIDE	DAYS TO GERMINATION

LIGHT NEEDS	SPACE REQUIREMENTS	PLANTING DATE	HARVESTING DATE	NOTES

67

PLANT NAME (and varietal)	SOURCE	PLANTING LOCATION	ANNUAL OR PERENNIAL	WHEN TO START SEEDS INSIDE	DAYS TO GERMINATION

LIGHT NEEDS	SPACE REQUIREMENTS	PLANTING DATE	HARVESTING DATE	NOTES

PLANT NAME (and varietal)	SOURCE	PLANTING LOCATION	ANNUAL OR PERENNIAL	WHEN TO START SEEDS INSIDE	DAYS TO GERMINATION

LIGHT NEEDS	SPACE REQUIREMENTS	PLANTING DATE	HARVESTING DATE	NOTES

PLANT NAME (and varietal)	SOURCE	PLANTING LOCATION	ANNUAL OR PERENNIAL	WHEN TO START SEEDS INSIDE	DAYS TO GERMINATION

LIGHT NEEDS	SPACE REQUIREMENTS	PLANTING DATE	HARVESTING DATE	NOTES

PLANT NAME (and varietal)	SOURCE	PLANTING LOCATION	ANNUAL OR PERENNIAL	WHEN TO START SEEDS INSIDE	DAYS TO GERMINATION

LIGHT NEEDS	SPACE REQUIREMENTS	PLANTING DATE	HARVESTING DATE	NOTES

PLANT NAME (and varietal)	SOURCE	PLANTING LOCATION	ANNUAL OR PERENNIAL	WHEN TO START SEEDS INSIDE	DAYS TO GERMINATION

LIGHT NEEDS	SPACE REQUIREMENTS	PLANTING DATE	HARVESTING DATE	NOTES

Part Four

WEEKLY
GARDENING JOURNAL

WEEK OF

TO-DO THIS WEEK

○ _____   ○ _____

○ _____   ○ _____

○ _____   ○ _____

○ _____   ○ _____

NOTES

_____

_____

_____

_____

_____

_____

WHY DO YOU WANT TO HAVE A GARDEN?

WEEK OF

TO-DO THIS WEEK

- ○ _____
- ○ _____
- ○ _____
- ○ _____
- ○ _____
- ○ _____
- ○ _____
- ○ _____

NOTES

_____

_____

_____

_____

_____

_____

I go to nature to be soothed and healed, and to have my senses put in order.

—JOHN BURROUGHS

WEEK OF

TO-DO THIS WEEK

○ _____ ○ _____

○ _____ ○ _____

○ _____ ○ _____

○ _____ ○ _____

NOTES

_____

_____

_____

_____

_____

_____

DO YOU HAVE A LOCAL GARDEN THAT YOU LOVE TO VISIT?
IS THERE ANYTHING YOU CAN REPLICATE FOR YOUR OWN GARDEN?

_____

_____

_____

_____

_____

WEEK OF

TO-DO THIS WEEK

○ _____   ○ _____

○ _____   ○ _____

○ _____   ○ _____

○ _____   ○ _____

NOTES

_____

_____

_____

_____

_____

_____

Green is the prime color of the world, and that from which its loveliness arises.

—PEDRO CALDERÓN DE LA BARCA

WEEK OF

TO-DO THIS WEEK

- ○ _____
- ○ _____
- ○ _____
- ○ _____

- ○ _____
- ○ _____
- ○ _____
- ○ _____

NOTES

_____

_____

_____

_____

_____

_____

WHAT DO YOU WANT FROM YOUR OUTDOOR SPACE?

_____

_____

_____

_____

_____

WEEK OF

TO-DO THIS WEEK

○ _____   ○ _____

○ _____   ○ _____

○ _____   ○ _____

○ _____   ○ _____

NOTES

_____

_____

_____

_____

_____

_____

All things great are wound up
with all things little.

—L.M. MONTGOMERY

WEEK OF

TO-DO THIS WEEK

- ○ _____
- ○ _____
- ○ _____
- ○ _____
- ○ _____
- ○ _____
- ○ _____
- ○ _____

NOTES

_____

_____

_____

_____

_____

_____

DO YOU HAVE ANY FAMILY MEMBERS OR FRIENDS WHO ARE WELL VERSED IN GARDENING? IF NOT, THINK ABOUT HOW YOU CAN GROW YOUR GARDENING COMMUNITY.

WEEK OF

TO-DO THIS WEEK

- ○ _____
- ○ _____
- ○ _____
- ○ _____
- ○ _____
- ○ _____
- ○ _____
- ○ _____

NOTES

_____
_____
_____
_____
_____
_____

Everything that slows us down and forces
patience, everything that sets us back
into the slow circles of nature, is a help.
Gardening is an instrument of grace.

—MAY SARTON

WEEK OF

TO-DO THIS WEEK

- ○ _____
- ○ _____
- ○ _____
- ○ _____

- ○ _____
- ○ _____
- ○ _____
- ○ _____

NOTES

_____
_____
_____
_____
_____
_____

WHAT INSPIRED YOU TO GET INTO GARDENING?

WEEK OF

TO-DO THIS WEEK

- ○ _____
- ○ _____
- ○ _____
- ○ _____

- ○ _____
- ○ _____
- ○ _____
- ○ _____

NOTES

_____

_____

_____

_____

_____

_____

The beauteous pansies rise
In purple, gold, and blue,
With tints of rainbow hue
Mocking the sunset skies.

—THOMAS J. OUSELEY

WEEK OF

TO-DO THIS WEEK

- ○ _____
- ○ _____
- ○ _____
- ○ _____

- ○ _____
- ○ _____
- ○ _____
- ○ _____

NOTES

_____
_____
_____
_____
_____
_____

WHICH PLANTS BRING YOU THE MOST JOY? LIST THEM HERE.

WEEK OF

TO-DO THIS WEEK

- ○ _____
- ○ _____
- ○ _____
- ○ _____
- ○ _____
- ○ _____
- ○ _____
- ○ _____

NOTES

_____
_____
_____
_____
_____
_____
_____

Won't you come into the garden? I would like my roses to see you.

—RICHARD BRINSLEY SHERIDAN

WEEK OF

TO-DO THIS WEEK

○ _____   ○ _____

○ _____   ○ _____

○ _____   ○ _____

○ _____   ○ _____

NOTES

_____

_____

_____

_____

_____

_____

_____

WHAT WAS YOUR FIRST GARDENING SUCCESS?

WEEK OF

TO-DO THIS WEEK

- ○ _____
- ○ _____
- ○ _____
- ○ _____
- ○ _____
- ○ _____
- ○ _____
- ○ _____

NOTES

_____

_____

_____

_____

_____

_____

For the things we have to learn
before we can do them, we learn
by doing them.

—ARISTOTLE

WEEK OF

TO-DO THIS WEEK

○ _____   ○ _____

○ _____   ○ _____

○ _____   ○ _____

○ _____   ○ _____

NOTES

_____

_____

_____

_____

_____

_____

_____

RESEARCH PLANTS NATIVE TO YOUR AREA. ARE THERE ANY YOU WANT TO GROW IN YOUR GARDEN?

WEEK OF

TO-DO THIS WEEK

- ○ _____
- ○ _____
- ○ _____
- ○ _____
- ○ _____
- ○ _____
- ○ _____
- ○ _____

NOTES

_____
_____
_____
_____
_____
_____
_____

Flowers always make people better, happier, and more helpful; they are sunshine, food, and medicine for the soul.

—LUTHER BURBANK

WEEK OF

TO-DO THIS WEEK

○ _____   ○ _____

○ _____   ○ _____

○ _____   ○ _____

○ _____   ○ _____

NOTES

_____

_____

_____

_____

_____

_____

_____

WHAT IS YOUR GOAL FOR THIS YEAR'S GARDEN?

WEEK OF

TO-DO THIS WEEK

- ○ _____
- ○ _____
- ○ _____
- ○ _____

- ○ _____
- ○ _____
- ○ _____
- ○ _____

NOTES

_____
_____
_____
_____
_____
_____

If you have a garden and a library, you have everything you need.

—MARCUS TULLIUS CICERO

WEEK OF

TO-DO THIS WEEK

○ _____   ○ _____

○ _____   ○ _____

○ _____   ○ _____

○ _____   ○ _____

NOTES

_____

_____

_____

_____

_____

_____

WHAT'S SOMETHING NEW THAT YOU OBSERVED THIS WEEK IN YOUR OUTDOOR SPACE?

_____

_____

_____

_____

_____

WEEK OF

TO-DO THIS WEEK

○ _____   ○ _____

○ _____   ○ _____

○ _____   ○ _____

○ _____   ○ _____

NOTES

_____

_____

_____

_____

_____

_____

A garden to walk in and immensity to dream in—what more could he ask? A few flowers at his feet and above him the stars.

—VICTOR HUGO

WEEK OF

TO-DO THIS WEEK

○ _____   ○ _____

○ _____   ○ _____

○ _____   ○ _____

○ _____   ○ _____

NOTES

_____

_____

_____

_____

_____

_____

_____

WHAT ARE YOU MOST EXCITED ABOUT FOR THIS SEASON?

WEEK OF

TO-DO THIS WEEK

○ _____ ○ _____

○ _____ ○ _____

○ _____ ○ _____

○ _____ ○ _____

NOTES

_____

_____

_____

_____

_____

_____

Help us to be ever faithful gardeners of the spirit, who know that without darkness nothing comes to birth, and without light nothing flowers.

—MAY SARTON

WEEK OF

TO-DO THIS WEEK

○ _____   ○ _____

○ _____   ○ _____

○ _____   ○ _____

○ _____   ○ _____

NOTES

_____

_____

_____

_____

_____

_____

WHAT HAVE YOU LEARNED SO FAR?

_____

_____

_____

_____

_____

WEEK OF

TO-DO THIS WEEK

- ○ _____
- ○ _____
- ○ _____
- ○ _____
- ○ _____
- ○ _____
- ○ _____
- ○ _____

NOTES

_____
_____
_____
_____
_____
_____
_____

Who loves a garden loves a greenhouse too.

—WILLIAM COWPER

WEEK OF

TO-DO THIS WEEK

○ _____   ○ _____

○ _____   ○ _____

○ _____   ○ _____

○ _____   ○ _____

NOTES

_____

_____

_____

_____

_____

_____

DESCRIBE HOW YOUR GARDEN MAKES YOU FEEL.

_____

_____

_____

_____

_____

WEEK OF

TO-DO THIS WEEK

○ _____   ○ _____

○ _____   ○ _____

○ _____   ○ _____

○ _____   ○ _____

NOTES

_____

_____

_____

_____

_____

_____

Weeds are flowers too, once you get to know them.

—A. A. MILNE

WEEK OF

TO-DO THIS WEEK

○ _____   ○ _____

○ _____   ○ _____

○ _____   ○ _____

○ _____   ○ _____

NOTES

_____

_____

_____

_____

_____

_____

IS ANYTHING STRUGGLING? IF SO, THINK ABOUT WHAT COULD BE HINDERING THE PLANT'S GROWTH.

WEEK OF

TO-DO THIS WEEK

- ○ _____
- ○ _____
- ○ _____
- ○ _____

- ○ _____
- ○ _____
- ○ _____
- ○ _____

NOTES

_____

_____

_____

_____

_____

_____

From plants that wake when others sleep,
From timid jasmine buds that keep
Their odor to themselves all day
But when the sunlight dies away
Let the delicious secret out
To every breeze that roams about.

—THOMAS MOORE

WEEK OF

TO-DO THIS WEEK

○ _____   ○ _____

○ _____   ○ _____

○ _____   ○ _____

○ _____   ○ _____

NOTES

_____

_____

_____

_____

_____

_____

DELIGHT IN YOUR SENSES THIS WEEK. WHAT DO YOU MOST LIKE TO SEE, HEAR, TOUCH, SMELL, AND TASTE IN YOUR GARDEN?

WEEK OF

TO-DO THIS WEEK

○ _____   ○ _____

○ _____   ○ _____

○ _____   ○ _____

○ _____   ○ _____

NOTES

_____

_____

_____

_____

_____

_____

_____

Anyone who stops learning is old, whether at twenty or eighty.

—HENRY FORD

WEEK OF

TO-DO THIS WEEK

○ _____   ○ _____

○ _____   ○ _____

○ _____   ○ _____

○ _____   ○ _____

NOTES

_____

_____

_____

_____

_____

_____

LIST THREE WORDS THAT DESCRIBE HOW GARDENING MAKES YOU FEEL.

_____

_____

_____

_____

_____

_____

WEEK OF

TO-DO THIS WEEK

○ _____   ○ _____

○ _____   ○ _____

○ _____   ○ _____

○ _____   ○ _____

NOTES

_____

_____

_____

_____

_____

_____

_____

Plant and your spouse plants
with you; weed and you
weed alone.

—JEAN-JACQUES ROUSSEAU

WEEK OF

TO-DO THIS WEEK

- ○ _____
- ○ _____
- ○ _____
- ○ _____
- ○ _____
- ○ _____
- ○ _____
- ○ _____

NOTES

_____
_____
_____
_____
_____
_____
_____

WHAT'S GROWING WELL THIS WEEK?

WEEK OF

TO-DO THIS WEEK

○ _____   ○ _____

○ _____   ○ _____

○ _____   ○ _____

○ _____   ○ _____

NOTES

_____

_____

_____

_____

_____

_____

And forget not that the earth
delights to feel your bare feet
and the winds long to play with
your hair.

—KHALIL GIBRAN

WEEK OF

TO-DO THIS WEEK

- ○ _____
- ○ _____
- ○ _____
- ○ _____
- ○ _____
- ○ _____
- ○ _____
- ○ _____

NOTES

_____
_____
_____
_____
_____
_____
_____

HAVE YOU OBSERVED ANY POLLINATORS AND BENEFICIAL INSECTS IN YOUR
GARDEN? HOW ABOUT PESTS?

WEEK OF

TO-DO THIS WEEK

- ○ _____
- ○ _____
- ○ _____
- ○ _____

- ○ _____
- ○ _____
- ○ _____
- ○ _____

NOTES

_____

_____

_____

_____

_____

_____

A weed is but an unloved flower.

—ELLA WHEELER WILCOX

WEEK OF

TO-DO THIS WEEK

○ _____   ○ _____

○ _____   ○ _____

○ _____   ○ _____

○ _____   ○ _____

NOTES

_____

_____

_____

_____

_____

_____

OBSERVE THE DIVERSITY OF PLANTS IN YOUR GARDEN. HOW MANY DIFFERENT SPECIES CAN YOU DETECT?

WEEK OF

TO-DO THIS WEEK

- ○ _____
- ○ _____
- ○ _____
- ○ _____

- ○ _____
- ○ _____
- ○ _____
- ○ _____

NOTES

_____

_____

_____

_____

_____

_____

One's mind, once stretched by a new idea, never regains its original dimensions.

—OLIVER WENDELL HOLMES

WEEK OF

TO-DO THIS WEEK

○ _____ ○ _____

○ _____ ○ _____

○ _____ ○ _____

○ _____ ○ _____

NOTES

_____

_____

_____

_____

_____

_____

WHAT COULD USE A LITTLE MORE LOVE THIS WEEK IN THE GARDEN?

WEEK OF

TO-DO THIS WEEK

○ _____   ○ _____

○ _____   ○ _____

○ _____   ○ _____

○ _____   ○ _____

NOTES

_____

_____

_____

_____

_____

_____

_____

I want it said of me by those who knew me best, that I always plucked a thistle and planted a flower where I thought a flower would grow.

—ABRAHAM LINCOLN

WEEK OF

TO-DO THIS WEEK

- ○ _____
- ○ _____
- ○ _____
- ○ _____

- ○ _____
- ○ _____
- ○ _____
- ○ _____

NOTES

HOW HAS YOUR GARDEN CHANGED SO FAR?

_____

_____

_____

_____

_____

WEEK OF

TO-DO THIS WEEK

- ○ _____
- ○ _____
- ○ _____
- ○ _____

- ○ _____
- ○ _____
- ○ _____
- ○ _____

NOTES

_____

_____

_____

_____

_____

_____

Gardens are not made by
singing 'Oh, how beautiful!'
and sitting in the shade.

—RUDYARD KIPLING

WEEK OF

TO-DO THIS WEEK

- ○ _____
- ○ _____
- ○ _____
- ○ _____
- ○ _____
- ○ _____
- ○ _____
- ○ _____

NOTES

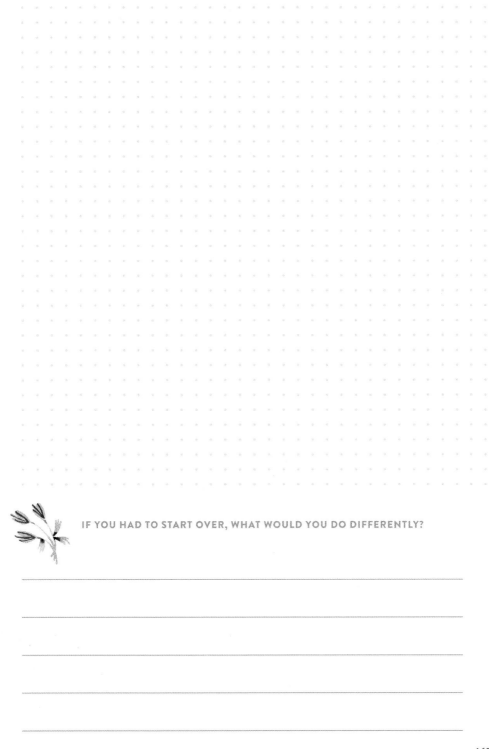

IF YOU HAD TO START OVER, WHAT WOULD YOU DO DIFFERENTLY?

WEEK OF

TO-DO THIS WEEK

- ○ _____
- ○ _____
- ○ _____
- ○ _____

- ○ _____
- ○ _____
- ○ _____
- ○ _____

NOTES

What is a weed? A plant whose virtues have never been discovered.

—RALPH WALDO EMERSON

WEEK OF

TO-DO THIS WEEK

○ _____   ○ _____

○ _____   ○ _____

○ _____   ○ _____

○ _____   ○ _____

NOTES

_____

_____

_____

_____

_____

_____

_____

WHAT HAS MOST SURPRISED YOU WITH THIS SEASON'S GARDEN?

WEEK OF

TO-DO THIS WEEK

○ _____ ○ _____

○ _____ ○ _____

○ _____ ○ _____

○ _____ ○ _____

NOTES

_____

_____

_____

_____

_____

_____

Delicious autumn! My very soul is wedded to it, and if I were a bird I would fly about the Earth seeking the successive autumns.

—GEORGE ELIOT

WEEK OF

TO-DO THIS WEEK

○ _____ ○ _____

○ _____ ○ _____

○ _____ ○ _____

○ _____ ○ _____

NOTES

_____

_____

_____

_____

_____

_____

WHAT KIND OF MAINTENANCE WILL YOUR GARDEN NEED NEXT SEASON?

WEEK OF

TO-DO THIS WEEK

○ _____   ○ _____

○ _____   ○ _____

○ _____   ○ _____

○ _____   ○ _____

NOTES

_____

_____

_____

_____

_____

_____

Autumn is the mellower season, and what we lose in flowers we more than gain in fruits.

—SAMUEL BUTLER

WEEK OF

TO-DO THIS WEEK

○ _____   ○ _____

○ _____   ○ _____

○ _____   ○ _____

○ _____   ○ _____

NOTES

_____

_____

_____

_____

_____

_____

_____

DID YOU OPTIMIZE THE AVAILABLE SPACE FOR YOUR GARDEN?

WEEK OF

TO-DO THIS WEEK

○ _____   ○ _____

○ _____   ○ _____

○ _____   ○ _____

○ _____   ○ _____

NOTES

_____

_____

_____

_____

_____

_____

We can do anything we want to if we stick to it long enough.

—HELEN KELLER

WEEK OF

TO-DO THIS WEEK

○ _____ ○ _____

○ _____ ○ _____

○ _____ ○ _____

○ _____ ○ _____

NOTES

_____

_____

_____

_____

_____

_____

WHAT ARE YOUR GOALS FOR NEXT SEASON?

WEEK OF

TO-DO THIS WEEK

- ○ _____
- ○ _____
- ○ _____
- ○ _____
- ○ _____
- ○ _____
- ○ _____
- ○ _____

NOTES

_____
_____
_____
_____
_____
_____

Garden as though you will live forever.

—WILLIAM KENT

ADDITIONAL RESOURCES

BOOKS

- *Grow and Gather: A Gardener's Guide to a Year of Cut Flowers* by Grace Alexander

- *Biodynamic Gardening: Grow Healthy Plants and Amazing Produce* by Monty Waldin

- *All New Square Foot Gardening, 3rd Edition* by Mel Bartholomew with The Square Foot Gardening Foundation

- *Braiding Sweetgrass: Indigenous Wisdom, Scientific Knowledge, and the Teachings of Plants* by Robin Wall Kimmerer

- *High-Yield Vegetable Gardening: Grow More of What You Want in the Space You Have* by Colin McCrate and Brad Halm

SEED COMPANIES

- Brecks (Flowers)

- Botanical Interests (High-quality seeds and garden products)

- Kitazawa Seed Co. (Traditional heirloom Asian vegetables)

- "Floret Flower Farm (high quality, unique heirloom flower seeds)"

- Baker Creek Seeds (Unique heirloom vegetable and flower varietals)

- Schreiner's Iris Gardens (Heirloom irises)

- Seed Savers Exchange (The world's largest seed exchange)

OTHER HELPFUL TOOLS

- PlantNet (A phone app to help you identify plants)
- The Farmer's Almanac Garden Planner (A useful tool that will help you digitally lay out and plan your garden)

SOIL RESOURCES

- Black Gold® (Natural and organic potting mixes and soil amendments)
- FoxFarm's Ocean Forest® Potting Soil (Nutrient-rich potting soil that contains earthworm castings and bat guano)
- Dr. Earth Potting Soil (Soil for both outdoor and indoor container gardening)
- Good Dirt (Sustainable-packaged soil and fertilizers)

GREAT GARDENERS TO FOLLOW

- Erin Benzakein of Floret Flowers (@floretflower)
- Ron Finley (@ronfinleyhq)
- Linda Ly from Garden Betty (@gardenbetty)
- Nicole Johnsey Burke of Gardenary (@gardenaryco)
- Kevin Espiritu from Epic Gardening (@epicgardening)

ABOUT THE AUTHORS

Sarah and Colin Simon, the husband and wife duo behind *My Gardening Journal*, find inspiration for all their creative projects in their ever-blooming Seattle-based urban farm. Sarah, world-renowned painting instructor and creator of the international best-selling *Watercolor Workbook* series, has taught thousands of budding artists the joy of creating lush watercolors inspired by the diverse variety of flowers, trees, and herbs grown in their garden. Colin, wealth advisor by day and steadfast gardener in every other waking moment, is the backbone of their garden, nurturing annual and perennial plants while also exploring unique, heirloom varieties in their greenhouse. Having grown up gardening with his mother and grandfather, he's acquired decades of gardening experience and wisdom, nurturing a devotion to growing beautiful plants. Together, Sarah and Colin are passionate about teaching others the value of patience, diligence, and curiosity in their approaches to gardening. The couple and their two daughters split their time between Seattle, Washington and Charleston, South Carolina, tending to their robust gardens at both homes.

Paige Tate & Co.

Copyright © 2023 Sarah Simon

Published by Paige Tate & Co.

Paige Tate & Co. is an imprint of Blue Star Press

PO Box 8835, Bend, OR 97708

contact@paigetate.com

www.paigetate.com

Designed by Brooke Johnson

Production Design by The Sly Studio

Photography by Stephanie Bailey

ISBN: 9781941325957

Printed in Colombia

10 9 8 7 6 5 4 3 2